CONTENTS

Published in 2023 by Orange Mosquito
An Imprint of Welbeck Children's Limited
part of Welbeck Publishing Group.
Based in London and Sydney.
www.welbeckpublishing.com

In collaboration with Mosquito Books Barcelona S.L.

© Mosquito Books Barcelona, SL 2022
Text © Lucas Riera 2022
Illustration © Grace Helmer 2022
Translation: Laura McGloughlin
Publisher: Margaux Durigon
Production: Jess Brisley

ISBN: 9781739099039
eISBN: 9781739099046

Printed in China
10 9 8 7 6 5 4 3 2 1

FSC
MIX
Paper
FSC® C020056

Lucas Riera • Grace Helmer

DOGS TO THE RESCUE!

True stories of canine heroes

ORANGE
M·O·S·Q·U·I·T·O

- Doberman
- Search and rescue, firefighter
- 5 years old

SURA

The search and rescue dog that looks for people

Sura is an air-scenting dog; this means that she doesn't follow tracks but instead detects the scent of human presence when there's been a landslide or an earthquake and people may be buried beneath the earth or in the rubble.

Who would have believed that the dog breed which Karl Friedrich Louis Dobermann created a century and a half ago to protect himself from thieves and assailants (he was a tax collector), would lead to a dog as elegant and effective as Sura. It seems incredible that a race famous for its fierceness can do such selfless work.

Sura is 5 years old and works with and is trained by John. For her it's a game, but the lives of people trapped with only minutes of air remaining depend on the speed of her work.

Did you know?

Dobermans are very energetic and smart dogs. They perform well in police and military work and one American Doberman named Kurt was the first dog buried in the US Marine Corps War Dog Cemetery.

- Border Collie
- Police Dog
- 9 years old

MIKI
The perfect tracker

Until the age of three and a half, Miki lived in an animal shelter...he was the wildest and most lively of all the dogs living there. He'd never sit still, was never satisfied, and needed constant stimulation. Then one day, a policeman was passing by the shelter and he noticed that Miki was an especially clever and quick dog. He adopted Miki and began to train him to pick up the trail of people who had disappeared.

Six years later Miki is a superstar and he never loses a trail, no matter how difficult it is. Not long ago he found a little boy whose body had been buried in the mountains. Miki's most recent feat was locating an old man who'd gone walking in the woods and had gotten lost: the man couldn't find his way back and he wasn't wearing a coat to protect him from the dropping temperatures. Miki saved his life.

- Labrador Retriever
- Therapy dog
- 8 years old

SOL
Fear-destroyer

Sol was a breeding dog living in a puppy mill. Her only function in life was to have puppies. The person who adopted her believes that Sol's had 100 or so puppies. At the puppy mill even though her basic needs were met—guaranteed food, shelter from the cold and rain, safety—Sol was permanently locked up. She'd never run freely through fields or smelled the scents of nature. She'd never been free to sniff a flower.

And even worse, no one had ever hugged Sol, or kissed her or cuddled her. She'd never stepped on sand on a beach or snow on a mountain. She didn't know how to swim and water terrified her.

Sol was adopted by Mary, who does animal-assisted therapy. She arrived at her new home cowering in fear and unease. She was so terrified that for the first few days she couldn't walk normally on the street and when she heard a car horn she wanted to run. It seemed she would never be able to overcome the enormous fears she felt. Poor Sol!

Little by little, with the help of her new family and their other dogs, Sol began to feel more secure and started enjoying life. Sol has now experienced the beach, snow, walks, roaming with the other dogs, and sometimes she helps bestow affection on people who, like her, have lived in situations where they've been afraid.

Today there is no one who can beat her swimming. As soon as she gets into the water she wants to stay there.

Did you know?

A labrador is a good-natured and hardworking dog, just like their ancestors who were historically used to help fishermen.

- Fox Terrier
- Assistance dog for seniors

MILO
Granny Pat's friend

Milo had a very hard childhood. She was tied to a chain for years. It is believed that some hunters kept her on their property along with another dog of the same breed, and once a week they'd put water and food within their reach.

A passerby noticed Milo's tragic situation and reported it to the police, who freed the poor little dog and brought her to an animal shelter to find her a new home.

Despite her history, Milo was very independent but she also loved people. Other maltreated dogs often displayed aggression towards humans—their abusers—but not Milo: as soon as anyone moved close to her, she snuggled up, demanding attention and giving lots of licks! Milo was very intelligent and very quick. Her favorite pastime was running at top speed through the countryside, chasing hares, wood mice, and whatever other animals she could detect.

Milo was so playful and determined that the first time she saw the sea she launched herself head-first into the water...what a fright! Her handler had to dive in after her so she wouldn't drown.

Despite being so active, Milo became friends with Pat, a very old lady who lived in an old people's home. Pat was unwell, and could barely move her hands because of osteoarthritis.

Pat was sad and felt she had no reason to keep living, and had already said she didn't want to do physical therapy exercises.

But Milo gave her so much energy and such a desire to keep enjoying life that Pat asked to start the rehabilitation program again: more than anything, she wanted to use her hands to stroke and groom Milo.

Pat spent her days smiling and thinking about seeing Milo, and the dog returned her feelings of unbreakable love.

Did you know?

The fox terrier was originally bred to flush foxes out of their hiding places during fox hunts.

- Mongrel
- Assistance dog for seniors
- 12 years old, retired

ARWEN

The dog full of pellets

Arwen was born with another name: she was called Minty. She belonged to a young couple who lived in Spain. When she was one year old, the couple decided to go and live in London, UK, for work reasons, and they abandoned her. That's a serious crime!

The poor, frightened dog lived alone, wandering the streets for a long time until she was picked up by an animal shelter, over 250 miles from where she was born.

A few months later, Victoria decided to adopt her. Victoria changed Minty's name to Arwen because her white coat reminded her of a character in a film she'd just seen: The Lord of the Rings. At first Arwen didn't adapt to her new home: everything frightened her, she'd cry when she was alone, she wouldn't eat...but slowly Victoria and her family managed to make Arwen feel at home and loved and safe.

The first time Victoria took Arwen to the vet for a check-up they took an X-ray and discovered that her body contained hundreds of pellets; a terrible reminder of those days of her abandonment, when she'd been shot at many times and the lead pellets were still in her body!

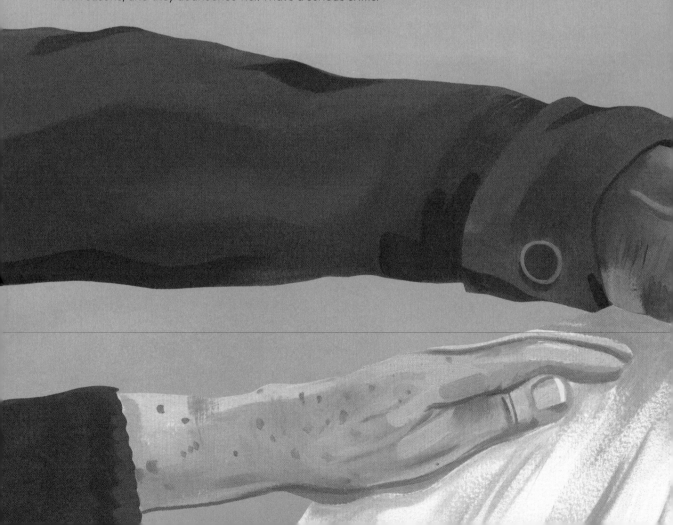

One day, Victoria decided to take Arwen to visit her elderly father, who lived in an old people's home. As they walked through the garden at the home, lots of old people came over to greet Arwen and play with her. When Victoria's father met Arwen he was happier and more communicative than he'd ever been before.

While they were visiting at the home, Arwen noticed an old woman who could hardly move, sitting in a wheelchair watching her. Without a sound, she went over to the chair and stayed by the woman's side. Happy and grateful, the woman began stroking Arwen.

After this, Victoria decided she should professionally train Arwen so that she could become a therapy dog.

Today, Arwen is 12 and retired. She lives at home with her family. Throughout her life, Arwen has helped many people; even now, from time to time, she visits an old people's home to provide emotional support.

Did you know?

A mongrel is a type of mixed-breed dog, which doesn't belong to an officially recognized breed.

- Labrador retriever
- Rescue dog
- 12 years old

Everyone in Mexico knows Frida, the rescue dog that used neoprene (a type of protective fabric) boots and special glasses to protect her eyes when she was doing her job. She recently retired and lives in the country now, teaching her job to other young dogs. Frida has been decorated as a heroine by the Mexican Navy.

During the terrible earthquakes that destroyed Mexico City in 2017, soldiers were working against the clock, searching for possible survivors trapped in the rubble. They were always accompanied by Frida; with her incredible sense of smell she could detect and find humans who were alive.

FRIDA

The rescuer

Frida became so well-known that when she was brought to a rescue site, accompanied by her trainer, Israel, people felt more hopeful. "If Frida is here, she'll find the people who are missing," everyone would say.

Before retiring, Frida took part in 53 rescue operations. She traveled all over Mexico, Haiti, Guatemala, and Ecuador, and saved 12 people in total.

The images of Frida and her handler searching among the rubble of a school to find the survivors drew worldwide attention.

Frida is an idol in Mexico, so much so that there is a bronze statue of her in the state of Puebla.

- Bloodhound
- Search and rescue dog

INDY
The super-gifted dog

Ernest is a professional firefighter. He works all over the city of Barcelona, Spain, and is always accompanied by Indy, a bloodhound with almost magical abilities.

Ernest says that dogs are born blind, but with a very well-developed sense of smell; they perceive maternal milk by the smell, because they can't yet find it with their eyes. But if all dogs can smell a trail with such a masterful ability, then Indy surpasses them to an extraordinary level; he's able to follow the trail of someone who went somewhere many days before.

As a good search and rescue dog, Indy specializes in tracking people who have become lost and in finding those alive in floods, earthquakes, and other catastrophes.

Did you know?

The bloodhound's ancestors were created in medieval France to trail deer and boar..

- Mixed breeds
- Therapy dogs
- 12 years old

PRINCESS AND REY

The best of friends

Princess and Rey are like Siamese twins; while they have different temperaments, no one can separate them. However, they're not siblings by blood, but best friends. Rey is big, friendly, calm, and confident; when he sees a human, he goes over and offers himself as a playmate.

On the other hand, Princess is a little insecure, timid and wary of everyone at first, but then she's a delight. Her foster parent thinks that perhaps she had some bad experiences in the past.

After a few weeks of living in their foster parent's house, Princess and Rey found a new home . . . in jail!

From the dogs' first day in the prison, the inmates were delighted with Princess and Rey. They could see immediately that Princess was less sociable and more timid than Rey and they helped her integrate. Very soon, Princess and Rey began to change the prisoners' behavior.

Conduct hugely improved, communal living even more so, and no one wanted to miss an opportunity to be with the dogs, walking them, caring for them, and keeping them company.

Anthony was a famous bank robber. He'd spent his whole life going in and out of jail. As soon as he was released, he'd start planning another hold-up. Anthony said he didn't know how to do anything else and was sure he was going to die in jail.

But Anthony and the two dogs became friends, close friends, the best of friends. Anthony began to have fewer conflicts with other inmates, and he was eventually trusted to become Princess and Rey's caretaker.

Years passed and the friendship grew so strong that when Anthony was on the verge of walking free, he asked the jail board to let him take Princess and Rey, who had already retired, with him so

they could spend their remaining years of life in a free, natural environment.

Today Anthony lives in an animal rehabilitation center with Princess and Rey...he has rebuilt his life with his new family and animals and has never thought about robbing a bank again.

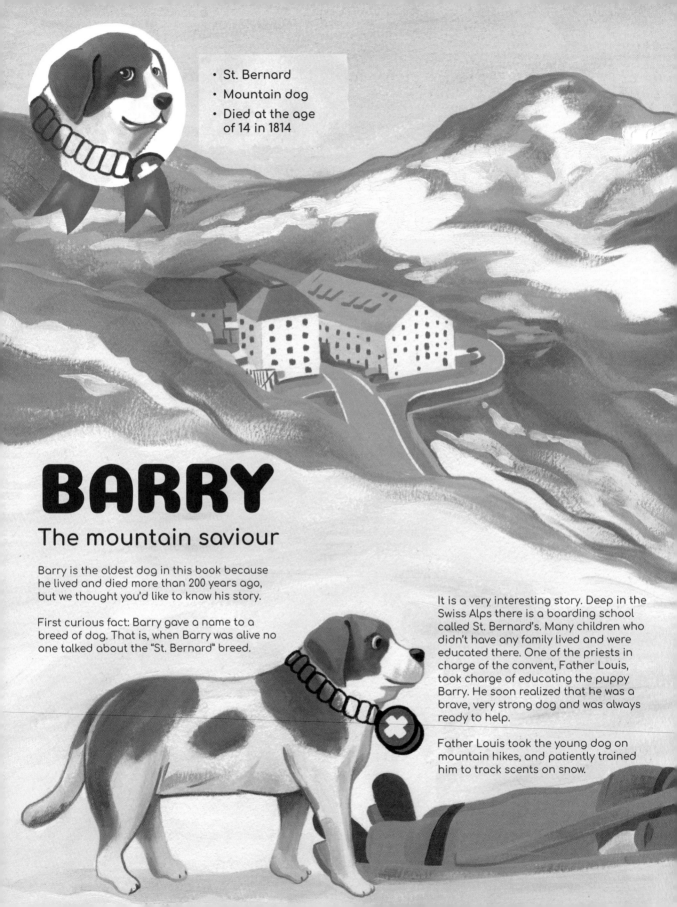

- St. Bernard
- Mountain dog
- Died at the age of 14 in 1814

BARRY

The mountain saviour

Barry is the oldest dog in this book because he lived and died more than 200 years ago, but we thought you'd like to know his story.

First curious fact: Barry gave a name to a breed of dog. That is, when Barry was alive no one talked about the "St. Bernard" breed.

It is a very interesting story. Deep in the Swiss Alps there is a boarding school called St. Bernard's. Many children who didn't have any family lived and were educated there. One of the priests in charge of the convent, Father Louis, took charge of educating the puppy Barry. He soon realized that he was a brave, very strong dog and was always ready to help.

Father Louis took the young dog on mountain hikes, and patiently trained him to track scents on snow.

St. Bernard's boarding school was located in a pass between Italy and Switzerland so many travelers and hikers would visit the area. Avalanches were not uncommon in the mountains and unfortunately, sometimes travelers got buried under the snow.

Barry would gaze at the mountain every day and without being told he would run toward it when he thought someone might be in trouble. Often on his own he'd find someone on the verge of dying and pull them from the snow. When he couldn't do it alone, he'd run back to the convent looking for Father Louis and the other children for them to come and help him.

It's said that before retiring Barry saved more than 40 people throughout his life. One of the loveliest stories is the one that tells how one day he found a little boy stranded in a cave of ice. First he dragged him out into the open air, licked him until he became warmer, and then he managed to get the poor little child onto his back and carried him to the convent.

To this day, there has always been a dog named Barry in the St. Bernard convent.

Did you know?

The Saint Bernard were originally bred for rescue work in the mountains. This dog is usually represented with a small barrel of brandy (an alcoholic drink) around its neck.

- German wire-haired pointer
- Police dog

TERRY
Always playing

Originally, pointers were bred as falcon hunters, but Terry works as a police dog and specializes in detecting drugs. His handler and trainer is an agent named George who never ceases to be amazed by his dog's abilities. One day they were both patrolling around a station, a place jammed with people coming and going. Suddenly, Terry pulled on the leash and casually went to sit down, without barking, on a traveler's suitcase. The man was a drug dealer who was carrying the

"merchandise" inside a vacuum-packed plastic bag, inside his suitcase!

If you ask George how Terry manages to detect drugs, he will tell you that he does it by playing. It's like a very fun and exciting competition for him and that's why he concentrates; he wants to win the prize his handler will give him, which is a chew toy.

Did you know?

Pointers' excellent noses and stamina are appreciated by hunters worldwide and they can retrieve any game from land or water.

- Mixed breed
- Therapy dog
- 10 years old.

PIPA
The puppy thrown in the bin

Someone threw Pipa into the trash and ran away. Can you imagine anything more cruel? Luckily a few hours later, and before the enormous and terrifying garbage truck came, someone heard her barks and yelps and rescued Pipa.

They took her to an animal shelter to recover. Despite her experience, Pipa still loved being around people and playing games with them.

Pipa was lucky because a family adopted her a few days later. She seemed to settle well in her new home. Then one night the family heard her yelping. They went down to where she slept and...surprise! Pipa had had six puppies.

Once Pipa had recovered and the puppies had been found safe homes, Pipa began to train to be a therapy dog.

Maria was a sad, insecure, depressive girl. She believed she wasn't worth anything and that her life had no meaning. She had even thought of ending her life, given that she couldn't find a reason to keep living . . . until one day she met Pipa.

Pipa was a very special, intelligent, and obedient therapy dog, she stayed by people's side, as long as they treated her well. As soon as she noticed something wasn't right, she would immediately leave, with no hesitation.

Maria learned that looking after Pipa was a good reason to get up every morning. Not only that; beginning to look after Pipa also helped her change her attitude toward her own life and she stopped being so sad. Little by little, her life began to have meaning.

When Maria left the therapy center, she wrote a beautiful card to the staff who had taken care of her, thanking them for their support and promising them that she would never forget Pipa.

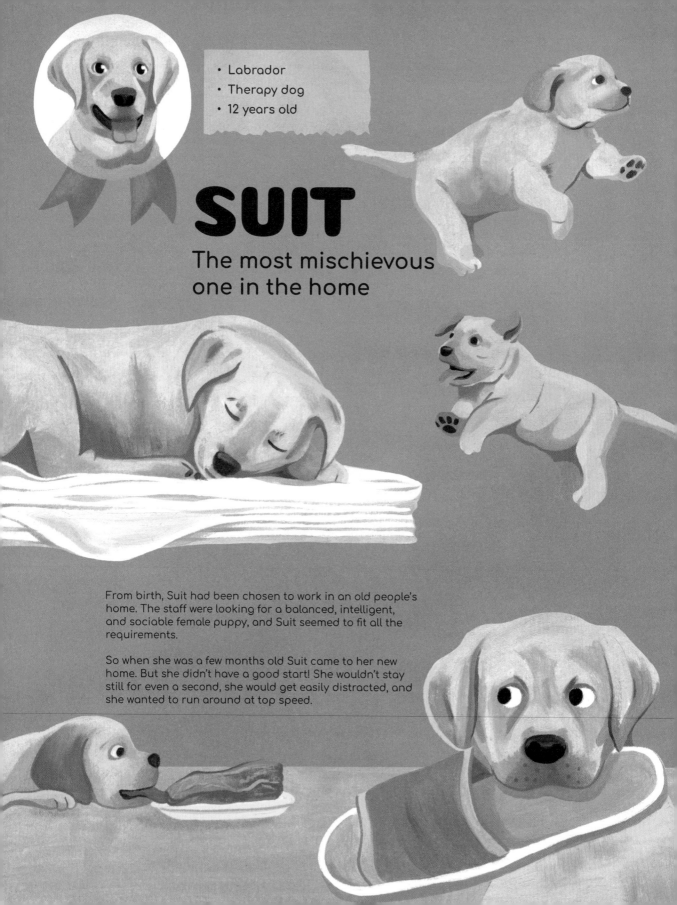

- Labrador
- Therapy dog
- 12 years old

SUIT
The most mischievous one in the home

From birth, Suit had been chosen to work in an old people's home. The staff were looking for a balanced, intelligent, and sociable female puppy, and Suit seemed to fit all the requirements.

So when she was a few months old Suit came to her new home. But she didn't have a good start! She wouldn't stay still for even a second, she would get easily distracted, and she wanted to run around at top speed.

And not only that; she was always getting into mischief. One day she robbed an old lady's slipper to play with it; another day she took a nap among freshly washed sheets; and on another afternoon she was found devouring a delicious piece of meat the cook had kept for dinner. But despite this, Suit was a lovely puppy. She was affectionate toward all the old people, and they were besotted with her.

David was the resident physical therapist. He helped the old people to keep fit through exercise and stretching. Only weeks after her arrival, Suit and David formed the perfect team. David had Suit accompany him to every session. It was fantastic; the old people responded well to Suit being in the sessions, and their progress noticeably improved.

One day while chasing a rabbit in the garden, Suit broke one of her paws. She had to rest and stop working for 2 months. Now it was the turn of the residents to visit the puppy and cheer her up! David helped her recovery a lot and their friendship grew even deeper.

When Suit retired, David managed to adopt her, and now they live as a family. Despite being retired, Suit loves visiting "her" residence.

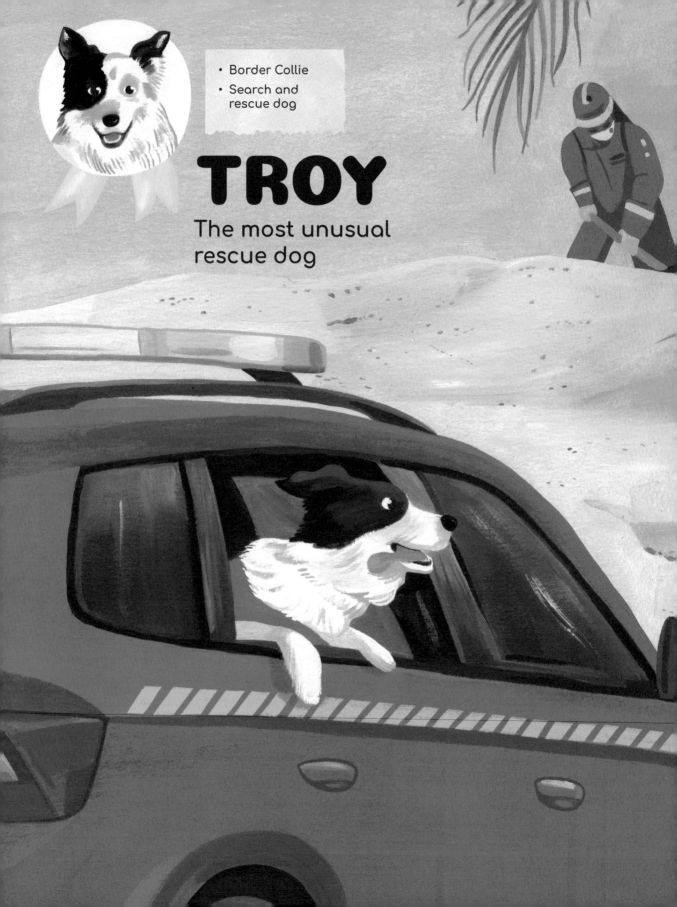

- Border Collie
- Search and rescue dog

TROY

The most unusual rescue dog

Troy is perhaps the most unusual search and rescue dog in history. Border collies are usually black with a white patch, but Troy is the exact opposite: white as snow, with a black patch around one eye.

Border collies are famous for being intelligent and good sheepdogs, and Troy is both of these things. However, to be a good search and rescue dog, Troy also has to be very obedient and he must not get nervous or scared; he must fulfill his instructor's orders perfectly, because someone's life may be at stake. Troy must also use his sense of smell to detect trapped, lost, or hidden people.

Troy has participated in many missions as a search and rescue dog. He loves going out in the K9 unit's car and helping people in trouble.

- Belgian Shepherd
- Police dog specialising in the fight against terrorism
- Died at the age of 7

DIESEL
Anti-terrorist hero

All police dogs do a heroic job, but those that specialize in the fight against terrorism are more worthy of praise than others because they risk their life during every operation.

So it was with Diesel, the Belgian shepherd dog that the French national police trained to detect explosives, pursue terrorists, and follow their tracks. He was a vital member of the elite police unit RAID, helping in the fight against terrorists.

Did you know?

The breed originated in Belgium where these dogs were used to herd sheep.

On one occasion, after causing various bombs to explode, some dangerous terrorists hid in an apartment near Paris. The police managed to locate them and began an operation to trap them. Diesel wasn't the only dog in the unit, but he was certainly the bravest.

Following a trace, Diesel succeeded in entering the apartment to signal to the police where the terrorists were hiding. But, after he entered, a bomb exploded. Diesel was struck by the full blast and tragically killed. However, his death saved many lives.

Some heroes sacrifice themselves so the rest of us can live safely and in peace, and no doubt Diesel was one of them.

- Airdale terrier
- Therapy dog
- 3 years old

SNOWY
No fear

Snowy was chosen as a therapy dog when she was 5 weeks old. Her trainers immediately saw that she was an animal with many qualities for helping others. But this doesn't mean she wasn't the naughtiest of her family.

She never stopped playing or running or sniffing around, and she was braver than anyone else. When she reached 6 months old, she damaged one of her teeth. The veterinarian told the family they had to make a decision; either her tooth had to be removed, or they could try to fix it with orthodontics.

And so Snowy wore braces, similar to the ones we humans use. After a month and a half she had completely recovered.

Did you know?

This dog breed originated in the Aire Valley of Yorkshire, UK, and was created to catch otters and rats.

Despite her energy and restlessness, Snowy is a dog who understands children very well. As she can do many tricks, like shake hands, play dead, and run between your legs, she immediately makes friends with young people.

In spite of her young age, Snowy has helped many children recover their self-esteem and overcome problems in relationships with others.

- Yorkshire terrier
- War and therapy dog
- Died at the age of 14 in 1957

If you think about a war dog, you'll imagine all kinds of animal...but not Smoky. He was a 6.5-inch-tall Yorkshire terrier that fitted inside the helmet of his friend and protector Bill Wynne, a photographer and combat pilot. Smoky's story is almost a legend. During World War II he was found by some American soldiers in New Guinea, and they took him with them. As he appeared not to understand anything, little by little they lost interest in the puppy, until they sold him to Bill Wynne who quickly saw that he was a prodigy of a dog.

What happened next has made Smoky and Bill famous all over the world. Smoky took part in 12 aerial missions at Bill's side. How incredible that a dog liked to fly so much!

SMOKY

War hero

But Smoky's greatest feat was something else entirely. When Bill's squadron was in the Philippines, the officials in charge needed to communicate with all their squadrons. To make this happen, they needed to run a cable underneath the landing strip of the airport. But they couldn't do the work because the enemy was watching the runway and shooting anything that moved.

Bill had a great idea. He thought that if he attached a cable to Smoky's collar and called him from the other side of the runway, the little dog would be able to go through the small drain and pull the communications cable through. The mission was a success! And it is believed that these communications saved hundreds of lives.

Did you know?

These little dogs are commonly referred as "Yorkies" and they got their name from their origin in Yorkshire, England.

Smoky has another distinction. When the war was over and he grew old, his greatest joy was being in hospitals keeping wounded soldiers company. Because of this, it's said that Smoky was the first therapy dog in history.

If you go to Cleveland, USA, be sure to visit the monument of Smoky sitting inside a helmet constructed by war veterans.

- Spanish water dog
- Police tracker dog
- 8 years old

TARA

The most sensitive sense of smell

Despite his shaggy appearance, Tara is an expert in detecting all kinds of explosives, one of the most delicate and difficult specialties there is.

Luckily, the objects these expert tracker dogs find almost never explode. Locating the explosives is vital and thanks to dogs like Tara many lives are saved.

Tara has to remember how each component of an explosive smells to detect them at any time and in any place.

Akira and the other trainers of the Police K9 Unit spend many hours training the dogs and deciding each one's best skill.

To give you an idea of how difficult this profession is, we can tell you that they select only 5% of the dogs they train. The rest go on to be adopted by families; they are very intelligent but not quite enough to be police dogs.

Did you know?

Water dogs once served as crew on fishing trips, herding fish into nets. They have webbed feet, which makes them great swimmers.

- Labrador Retriever
- Therapy dog
- Died at the age of 9

BEAU

Friendly giant

Saving the life of someone buried under the ground is a heroic act; likewise, detecting a hidden explosive and risking your life until it's successfully deactivated can only be done by the bravest of the brave.

But what about therapy dogs? These incredible dogs help people overcome their problems. They may not be well-known or appear on TV, but they too save lives. As in the case of Beau, a huge black pooch and specialist in therapy for troubled young people.

Ralph was one such troubled young man. He didn't fit in at the center where he lived and he found it

difficult to follow the rules. He was 15 when his parents lost custody of him, so along with other young boys he went to live in a center for minors. Ralph didn't like living there. His daily fights and conflicts with the other boys were constant and his way of solving problems had made him notorious among his companions as well as in the neighborhood. He seemed to be a bitter and angry young man.

One day, a big beautiful dog named Beau appeared. Ralph and Beau looked at one another and immediately connected. From then on Ralph's attitude began to change and he became happier, more friendly, and more considerate. Through Beau he learned how to relate better to his peers.

Ralph worked hard to treat his peers better and interact peacefully with others. Thanks to Beau and the link forged between them, he managed to find his path and improve on a personal level. Today Ralph is a young working man who has overcome his anger and bitterness.

- German Shepherd
- Police dog
- Died at the age of 12 in 2021

KITT

The ultimate police dog who gave his life for others

K9-Kitt spent 12 years working as a police dog. His human companion and trainer is named Bill. Both Kitt and Bill were well-trained to help their community. Bill trained Kitt every day for years to help in police prevention and surveillance work.

One day in early June, the police received a report of domestic violence; a man was attacking his wife. Bill, Kitt, and another official named Matthew hurried to the scene. They confronted a violent man who shot at them. Tragically, the two men were injured and Kitt was shot dead.

The police department organized a very moving homage to Kitt, the skilled police dog who fell in the line of duty. Sometimes, heroes like Kitt give their lives to protect others.

Did you know?

German shepherds have a long history of being featured in Hollywood movies!

HOW IS A HERO CHOSEN?

Isabel is a therapy dog specialist. And not only that; she loves dogs, cares for them, trains them, and shelters them at home if necessary. She is at the heart of a majority of the stories in this book; she's helped us a lot. One of Isabel's most important jobs is choosing which dogs can be therapy dogs. Only four or five out of every 100 dogs are suitable for this very important job.

Therapy dogs can be either puppies or adults and can come from not only breeders but animal protection shelters too. For example, one of the dogs you've met—Beau—passed four tests, like the others did. Isabel examined and tested 20 Labrador puppies, almost all of which were black.

FIRST TEST:

She observed how they played together and mixed with each other; she rejected the shyest and those most uneasy around others.

SECOND TEST:

By calling them softly, she checked which ones would make friends rapidly; she rejected the ones who didn't come to her.

THIRD TEST:

Handling test: She carefully picked up the puppies, caressed them, kissed them, and hugged them. The puppies that were most comfortable passed the test.

FOURTH TEST:

Recovery ability: When confronted with a noise or scary, unexpected situation, the puppies that recovered quickest were the ones chosen.

After all the tests, only Beau and one other puppy looked confidently and calmly at Isabel, waiting for more tests: these two puppies were going to be future therapy dogs.

Ten amazing facts about dogs

1 - Their sense of smell is so much better than ours: the area of cells in their brain that detect smells is around 40 times larger than for humans. That is why dogs are used to sniff out drugs, money, or people.

2 – Dogs can also be trained to sniff out medical conditions. Some of them can spot diseases, alert their owner, and sometimes flag when they need more medication.

3 – Dogs can sniff and breathe at the same time. Their noses are designed so smells can stay in their nose while air can move in and out of their lungs.

4 – Dogs can be excellent swimmers. Not all dogs like water but the ones who do can swim like champs! Just make sure you always keep an eye on them if they are in the water!

5 – Dogs can run really fast! The fastest breed of dog is the greyhound. These agile dogs can reach a top speed of 45mph.

6 – Dogs' nose prints are unique. Just like our fingerprints!

7 – Why are dog noses wet? It helps absorb scents and they understand a smell better by licking their nose.

8 – Dogs sweat through their paws. They don't sweat like we do and instead they pant to cool down.

9 – It seems that dogs can be left or right-pawed. Many studies show that they have a preferred paw.

10 – Dogs have a lot of muscles in their ears. They have around 18 muscles so they can capture sounds by moving their ears in different directions.